The NICKELS, DIMES, AND DOLLARS BOOK

A Wise Kid's Guide to Money Matters

by Ellen Sabin

and _____

WRITE YOUR NAME HERE

WATERING CAN® PRESS

www.wateringcanpress.com

WATERING CAN®

Growing Kids with Character

When you care about things and nurture them,
they will grow healthy, strong, and happy, and in turn,
they will make the world a better place.

All Watering Can Press titles are available at special quantity discounts for bulk purchases
for sales promotion, premiums, fund-raising, educational, or institutional use.

Watering Can Press offers customized versions of this book and will adjust content for use
by nonprofits and corporations in support of their community outreach and marketing goals.

**To inquire about bulk discounts or to learn more about customized book runs,
please visit our Web site or e-mail info@wateringcanpress.com.**

Text and illustrations © 2010 by Ellen Sabin

WATERING CAN is a registered trademark of Ellen Sabin.
Watering Can, New York, NY
Printed in China in August 2023

Written by Ellen Sabin
Illustrated by Kerren Barbas
Designed by Taryn Sefecka

ISBN: 978-0-9759868-9-9

Web site address: www.wateringcanpress.com

Dear _____,

Because I want you to have, enjoy, and feel good about money throughout your whole life, I am giving you this **NICKELS, DIMES, AND DOLLARS BOOK**.

As you use this book, you will learn smart ways to think about spending, sharing, saving, earning, and growing your money.

You will also see that the more you learn to manage your money, the more it will become something that can help you create a comfortable and meaningful future.

This is YOUR book. As the coauthor, you get to fill in the blanks, draw pictures, and collect ideas about all the ways you can make wise decisions about money matters.

When you make choices and develop habits that make you money-wise, you will be helping yourself and making me very proud of you.

From, _____

Some "thank-yous"

- To Taryn, Samantha, and Kerren; designer, editor, and illustrator. Their talents and contributions show that a final product is only as good as the sum of its parts.

- To my niece, Sydney, whose enjoyment of my first draft reaffirmed for me that a book teaching financial literacy could be fun and engaging for kids.

- To the educators, parents, and financial professionals whose input and expertise helped refine my message and words.

A NOTE TO ADULTS

The goal of this book is to teach children about money.
Even more so, it is to encourage children to develop money skills and habits that will lead them to be confident, responsible, balanced, and comfortable with money matters.

Through using this book, children will learn why and how to make thoughtful choices about spending, sharing, saving, earning, and growing money.

Along the way, this activity book will help children incorporate their values into their decision making, practice goal setting, and engage in activities that will make them feel proud of themselves.

Adults can join children in using this book. Even if children have the skills to read this book independently, they will benefit from your input, life experiences, and insights if you review this book with them.

Ultimately, I hope The NICKELS, DIMES, AND DOLLARS BOOK journey will help children develop healthy money habits that will have a positive impact on their character and well-being throughout their lives.

Table of Contents

Money is an important part of life.

Money lets people buy the things they need.

It also lets people buy the extra stuff that they want.

- When people have money, it can give them **opportunities and choices** in their lives. For example, having money can give people the opportunity to go to college, take a vacation, or live where they want.

- Having money can also help people be **independent**. That means that they can rely on themselves to get the things that they need.

- Making, saving, and sharing money often build **confidence**. They are accomplishments and can make people feel proud of themselves.

- Money also provides people with a **feeling of security**. When people have extra money set aside, they are more prepared for unexpected events. For example, if someone loses their job or if their car breaks down, having extra money will let that person handle their problem more easily.

- Money can also give people a powerful way to help **improve the lives of others** through charity.

As you can see, money can affect people's lives in many different ways.

As you get older, you'll be more and more in charge of your own money decisions. One day, you will earn money and make choices about how to spend, share, and save it.

Since you'll be handling money your entire life, it's a good idea to get smart about money matters now!

What are you waiting for? Turn the page and get started!

The Value of Money

Before we talk about the kind of money we use today, let's look back in history and learn why we use money in the first place.

A long time ago people didn't have money, but they did have needs. They needed food, shelter, and clothing.

So thousands of years ago, people traded the things they had (like food or fur) in exchange for the other things that they needed.

For example, a farmer who grew grapes might trade three bunches of grapes for a dozen apples from the apple farmer. Or a basket maker who needed shoes might trade two baskets for one pair of shoes from the shoemaker.

The key to trading (which is also called "bartering") was to decide the value of things. In our example, if everyone agreed that three bunches of grapes were worth a dozen apples, then there was a standard for "fair trades."

Visit the Trading Post on the next page. It's a place where you can think about what might make for fair trades. ➡

The Trading Post

Fill in the blanks below to see how YOU value different items and services.

Is there something that your sister, brother, or a friend has that you'd really like? What is it?_____

Now think of something you have that you'd be willing to give to them—and that you think they'd want—in exchange for that item.
What is it?_____

Is there a service you might like someone to do for you? Maybe reading to you, doing the dishes for you, or scratching your back?
What is it?_____

If someone does that for you, what service could you do for them in return? Some examples might be walking their dog or helping shovel snow.

_____

A fair trade would be this book_____for this book_____.
I would also trade this toy_____for this toy_____.
Now mix and match: I would trade this object (it can be a game, piece of clothing, or anything else)_____
for this other object_____.

So you see, trading is all about how people value different items
or services. People make trades when they feel that what they are giving
away is worth about the same amount as what they are getting.

The History of Currency

Now, let's get back to the history of money.

The barter system worked well if people traded similar goods, like in the case of the grape farmer and apple farmer. But what if the grape farmer didn't want apples and instead wanted wood to build a house? Trading got more and more complicated as people had more needs and wants.

To make exchanges easier, people invented the idea of using local items to represent something of value. These items became known as "currency," or money.

Cattle are the oldest of all forms of money ever used. Throughout history, people have also used beads, pebbles, spices, seashells, gold, teeth, and many other objects as their local currency.

As you can imagine, these items became tricky to use. Can you picture yourself carrying around a pocket full of teeth? So, over time, other forms of currency were created.

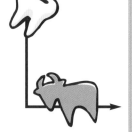

The very first coins invented were shaped like cattle. The value of these coins was based on their weight. That made it pretty hard to carry around a lot of money! Then the Greeks came up with the idea of making coins with their value printed on them. After that, paper money was invented in China.

Today, in most parts of the world, people use coins and paper money to buy and sell the things they need.

Currency Today

In the United States today we use coins and bills.
There are lots of cool things to learn about our currency!

We have six coins worth various amounts: the penny (one cent), the nickel (five cents), the dime (ten cents), the quarter (twenty-five cents), the half-dollar (fifty cents), and the silver dollar (one hundred cents).

We also have seven different bills. Did you know that each bill has a picture of someone on the front? Most of the people on our bills are former presidents, but not all of them. On the back of each of our bills there is an image of a famous building, monument, or scene from American history.

Here's a list of the bills we use in the United States today

Bill	Front	Back
$1	George Washington	Great Seal of the US
$2	Thomas Jefferson	The Declaration of Independence
$5	Abraham Lincoln	Lincoln Memorial
$10	Alexander Hamilton	US Treasury Building
$20	Andrew Jackson	White House
$50	Ulysses S. Grant	US Capitol
$100	Benjamin Franklin	Independence Hall

Money around the World

Almost every country has its own money.

Ask an adult for some help, or do some research, and see how many matches you can make between the countries listed below and their type of money.

COUNTRY	CURRENCY
INDIA	YEN
JAPAN	POUND
MEXICO	DOLLAR
ENGLAND	RUPEE
UNITED STATES	PESO
GERMANY	SHEKEL
ISRAEL	DIRHAM
MOROCCO	EURO

ANSWERS: India (Rupee); Japan (Yen); Mexico (Peso); England (Pound); United States (Dollar); Germany (Euro); Israel (Shekel); Morocco (Dirham)

Money in YOUR Pretend Country

The bills that are used around the world come in all sorts of different colors and sizes. They also show pictures of interesting people, places, and symbols.

If you were in charge of designing a bill for a new country, what would it look like?

Below, draw the front and back of your country's bill. If you want, you can include the amount your bill is worth, your country's name, pictures, sayings, colors, or anything else you can think of.

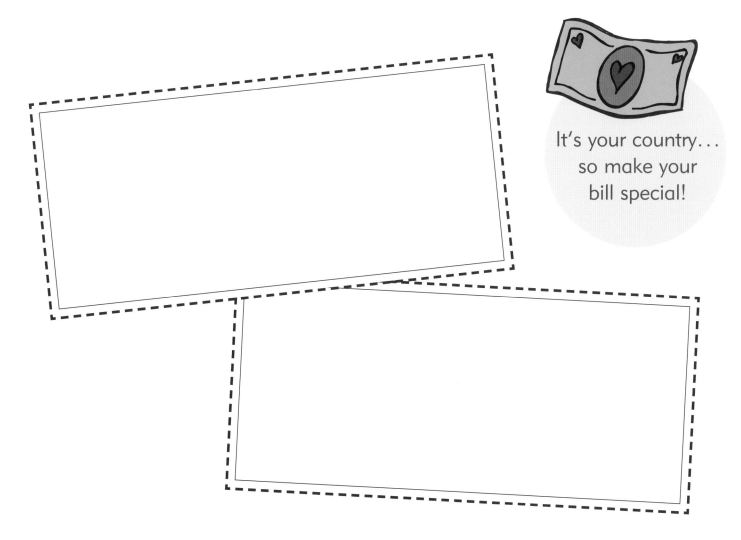

It's your country... so make your bill special!

Other Ways to Pay

A lot of the time, people use coins and bills to pay for what they buy.
But there are other ways to pay for things, too.

CHECKS

Checks are special pieces of paper from the bank. They are like a promise to pay someone. To use a check, the buyers write down the name of the person or store that they need to pay (the sellers) and the amount that they owe. Then the money is taken out of the buyers' bank accounts and put into the sellers' bank accounts. When people write checks, it's important that they have enough money in their bank accounts to keep their promises.

CREDIT CARDS

You've probably seen people paying for things with these plastic cards. When people use credit cards, they're actually borrowing money from a credit card company to buy their purchases. Then, at the end of the month, the credit card company adds up all the money that the buyers owe and sends them bills. The buyers then pay back the credit card company. When people use credit cards, it's important that they try to pay the company back on time. If they don't, they are charged extra money.

There are lots of good reasons to use checks and credit cards.
But it's smart to learn about careful and responsible ways to use them.

Talk to an adult and ask them if they have any advice about using checks and credit cards. If you learn something you want to remember, you can write it here:

....

....

You can learn even more about other ways to pay and money transactions if you ask them about debit cards, online banking, and ATMs.

The Mysteries of Money Quiz

How much do you really know about the money that's in your piggy bank?

Take this test and find out some wacky money facts.

1. How many times can a dollar bill be folded forward and backward before it tears?
a) 100
b) 4,000
c) 1,000,000

2. What was the largest US bill ever printed?
a) $1,000
b) $50,000
c) $100,000

3. What top-secret government agency was created to stop counterfeiters?
a) The Secret Service
b) The Postal Service
c) The Alien Squad

4. There is no such thing as a $2 bill.
a) True
b) False

5. If you made a row of pennies that was one mile long, how much money would you have?
a) $48.86
b) $844.80
c) $69,232.72

6. When US bills get too damaged to use, they are recycled into:
a) stationery
b) comic books
c) paper towels

7. Who was the first woman ever shown on US currency?
a) Rosa Parks
b) Sacagawea
c) Martha Washington

ANSWERS: 1. b) 4,000. 2. c) $100,000. This was never meant for people to use. It was only to make transfers between the Federal Reserve banks and the Treasury. 3. a) The Secret Service. 4. b) False. Since $2 bills are not printed very often, there are not too many in circulation. 5. b) $844.80. 6. a) stationery. 7. c) Martha Washington.

How do people get money?

WORK

Most adults have jobs to earn their money.

Most likely, your parent or caregiver goes to work every day so that he or she can make money.

In exchange for their time, energy, and ideas, he or she gets money in return. This is a modern-day version of a trade.

Your parent probably spends a lot of time at work. That's because he or she wants to be sure that you and your family have the money you need.

There are other ways people get money—like from gifts, inheritance, or investing—but mostly it's from work.

What can people DO with money?

Now that you know a bit about the value of money, the history of money, and how people get money, let's talk about what to DO with money.

Here are the things you can do with money:

SPEND IT

SHARE IT

SAVE IT

EARN IT

GROW IT

Wise Kids Manage Money

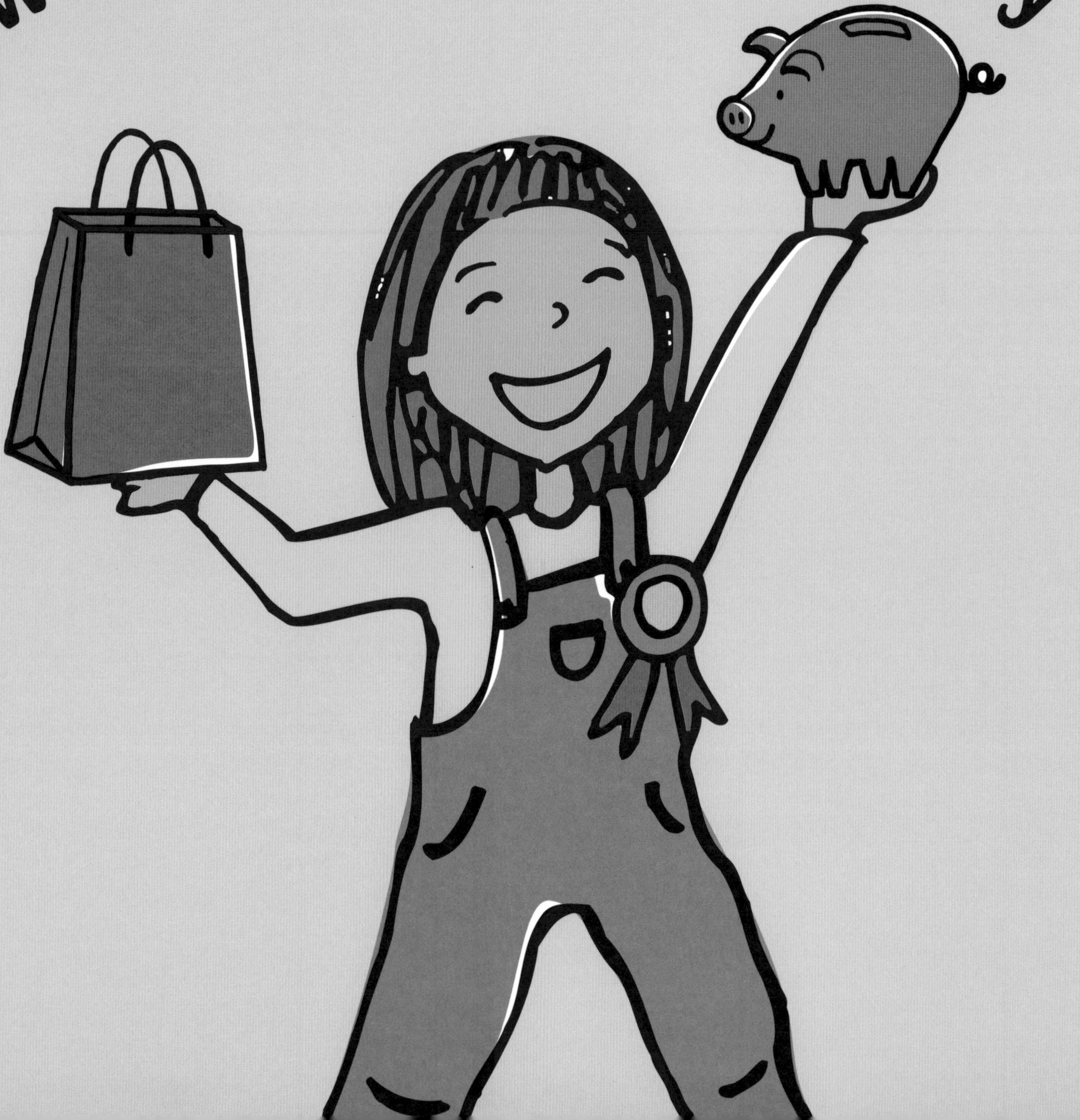

The most important thing you can learn about money is how YOU can manage it!

"Managing your money" means that you make careful plans and decisions about how and when to spend, share, save, earn, and grow your money.

A big part of managing money is finding a balance in how to use it. When someone creates a good balance for themselves, then they end up using money to make their life easier, nicer, and more meaningful.

Money will always have a big role in your life, but remember… money is just a thing. It's a tool for people to use to help them in their lives.

The more you learn to manage and enjoy money, the more it will be something that serves you!

Be the Boss of Your Money

It's important for people to first decide what they want to achieve with their money. Then they can make decisions and do things that make them the bosses and managers of their money.

People differ in what they want to achieve with their money. For example, some people want to have a lot of money to spend, while others feel better saving or sharing it. Some people want to work many hours to earn extra money, and others prefer to have less money and more free time.

The amount of money someone feels they need or want varies from person to person, but every adult needs some money. Not having enough money is really hard for people. But caring too much about money can also create problems. Each person eventually needs to decide how they want to live their life and what they want money to do for them.

What YOU end up doing with your money as you get older will be a personal decision. It should be guided by your values, goals, and future plans.

So on your path to becoming a wise money manager, you can start by thinking about your goals. Then you can make thoughtful plans and decisions that put—and keep—you in charge of your money.

MONEY BOSS!

What are some decisions YOU can make about money?

Pretend your mom or dad gives you $10 and says you can use it to buy whatever you want at the store.

What you decide to buy is a MONEY SPENDING DECISION.

Imagine that your family, classroom, or religious group gets together to raise money to give to a worthwhile cause. You get to help decide if the money goes to a charity that helps homeless people find homes, cleans up the environment, or takes care of sick animals.

What you choose is a MONEY GIVING DECISION.

If a family member gives you $20 for your birthday and says it's meant for you to save so you can use it in the future, what would you save it for?

That's a MONEY SAVING DECISION.

Think about something you really want, but you don't have quite enough money to buy. Now imagine that your sister has a lemonade stand and says you can help her and make some money. But what if it's a great day outside and you want to go play with friends? What would you do?

That's a MONEY MATTERS DECISION.

As you get older, these kinds of decisions will get bigger because you will be more and more in charge of your own money matters. But just like these examples, money decisions will always require you to think about your goals and values.

Goals and Planning

A goal is something that you want to achieve.

Some of your goals may have nothing to do with money. Maybe your goal is to write a book, learn to dive, or make a new friend.

Imagine that your goal is to become a great basketball player. To meet that goal, you'll need to practice really hard.

When you have a goal, there are always steps you need to take to get you there.

So, for example, to be a great basketball player, you may first need to learn how to dribble. That's a *short-term goal*. Once you are good at that and other skills, your next goal might be to make the basketball team. That's your *medium-term goal*. Way down the road, you may hope to play basketball in college or for a professional team. That's your *long-term goal*.

The things you do today, like practicing passing or your jump shot, will affect your short-term, medium-term, and long-term goals.

A Goal-Setting Exercise

Write down one of your personal goals below. It can be anything.
Think about something you want to learn, accomplish, create, or do.

What's your long-term goal? _____

Now follow the example about basketball and think of some steps that you can take to work toward achieving your goal.

What are some small things (your short-term goals) that you can do now to get closer to reaching that goal? _____

_____

_____

_____

What are some things you can do that might take a bit longer (your medium-term goals)? _____

_____

_____

_____

_____

Just think...the things you do today and tomorrow
will help you to meet your goals in the future!

Reaching Your Goals

What's the best way to reach your goals? **PLANNING!**

Once you know your goals,
the next step is to get planning.

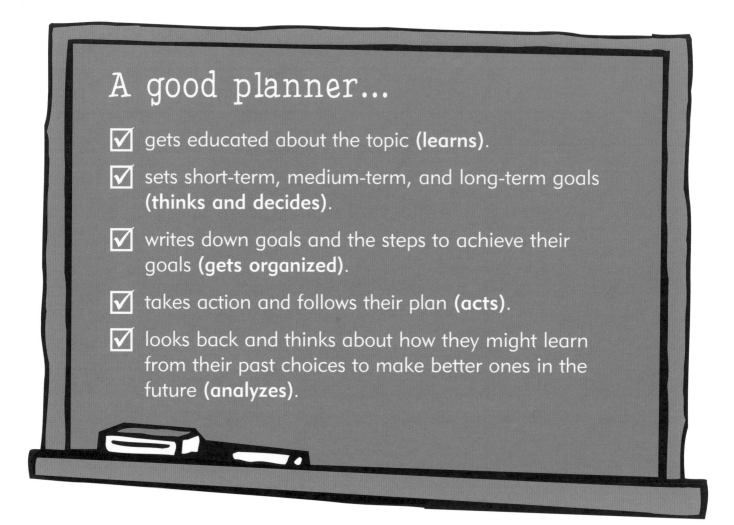

A good planner...

☑ gets educated about the topic (**learns**).

☑ sets short-term, medium-term, and long-term goals (**thinks and decides**).

☑ writes down goals and the steps to achieve their goals (**gets organized**).

☑ takes action and follows their plan (**acts**).

☑ looks back and thinks about how they might learn from their past choices to make better ones in the future (**analyzes**).

Money can help you reach some of your goals.

★ There are all different kinds of goals and even more ways to achieve them.

★ One useful tool that can help you reach your goals is money.

★ For example, money can help pay for lessons, books, supplies, or college.

★ Everyone has limits on how much money they have. And since people wish for lots of things that money can help them achieve, it's wise to learn how to be a smart money planner!

Money Planning

Just like planning for any goal, money planning means learning, thinking, deciding, getting organized, acting, and analyzing.

For money matters, there's a great tool to help you organize your planning. It's called a "budget."

A budget is a way to keep track of the money you get and the money you spend.

At the end of this book you are going to create your very own budget!

SPENDING MONEY

You can probably think of lots of things on which you and your family spend money. If you pay attention, you'll notice how often people spend money every day.

It's okay to spend money. It's also okay to enjoy spending money. And it's certainly good to enjoy the things you buy with your money.

The key to being a wise spender is to figure out what's worth spending your money on.

It's a good idea to first spend money on the things you need. Then you can spend money on the extra things you want. "Needs" are things you cannot manage without. "Wants" are things that you would like to have.

In this chapter, you will learn about making wise spending choices. You'll also get some ideas about how you can make your money go further by being a smart shopper.

Wants versus Needs

Pretend you are a parent and that you make all of the spending decisions for your family. You have a limited amount of money and you know it's smart to spend money on the things you and your family NEED before you spend money on the other things you WANT.

Circle the items below that you would consider NEEDS.

Music for your iPod

Money for electricity to light your house

Clothes to keep you and your kids warm

Books for your kids' school

Health care and medicine

New shoes to match your favorite dress

A place to live

A new painting for your house

A family vacation to Disneyland

A train/bus pass or car

Now, ask an adult in your family to help you make a list of other things that he or she considers needs. Write them here:

Making Choices and Setting Priorities

Knowing the difference between needs and wants will help you make important decisions about how to spend a limited amount of money.

Some people have extra money to spend on their wants. To figure out which of your wants to buy first, you need to think about your priorities—what is most important to you.

Practice setting spending priorities below.

First: Make a list of six things you wish you could buy now.

1. _____ ☐   4. _____ ☐

2. _____ ☐   5. _____ ☐

3. _____ ☐   6. _____ ☐

Next: Set your priorities! In the box next to each item, put a star, check, or X to show your choice.

Put a ⭐ next to the two items you want most. Those are your top priorities.

Put a ✔ next to the two items you want, but not quite as much as your top choices.

Put an ✘ next to the remaining two items. You still may want these things, but they are the least important to you.

You probably spend some money now, and you will certainly spend more money as you get older. It's smart to get in the habit of making a list—like this one—to help you think about your priorities before you use your money.

Smart Shopping

You've thought about what's really worth spending money on. Now it's time to think about wise shopping habits so that when you spend your money, you are making smart decisions!

Smart habits will help you spend less money and make your money go further.

1. Make a list. Before you go shopping, write down what you really want to buy. That way, when you are at the store and see lots of other things that look tempting to buy, you can look at your list and remember what you already decided you wanted.

2. Shop around and look for sales. Before you buy something, you and your mom or dad can look to see if it's being sold for less at a different store. If you do some research, you might find your item on sale.

3. Use coupons and discounts. Lots of times there are coupons in newspapers, at grocery stores, and on the Internet. Smart shoppers use these discounts to buy what they want for less money.

4. Find a bargain by being flexible. If you visit a discount store, sales rack, secondhand store, or yard sale, you might be able to find something similar to what you were looking for and at a cheaper price.

5. Enjoy shopping. Remember, having extra money is nice. So when you decide to spend it, have fun!

A Thoughtful Spending Exercise

Picture this: You live in a place that gets really cold in the winter. Usually, your mom or dad buys your clothes for you. However, this year you are given $100 and told that YOU will be in charge of making all of your own winter clothes spending decisions.

✓ Check off the items below that you want to buy. Don't forget to keep in mind your needs versus your wants and some of the smart shopping choices on the previous page. Remember, you only have $100. Be sure to pick wisely. Happy shopping!

Hopefully, you are proud of yourself for your smart spending choices, and you will be nice and warm all winter long.

A Wise Spending Checklist

Do you have an allowance or gift money that you'd like to spend? If so, that's great! It can be fun to spend money. It's also good practice, since you will be making spending decisions for your whole life.

When you spend money, there are some key things you can ask yourself to be sure that you are being a wise money manager.

Here are some questions that adults often ask themselves before they spend money. You will see that some of these questions are helpful—even at your age!

Will I still want this a week from now? A month from now?

Do I need this or want this?

Do I have enough money to buy it?

What things won't I be able to buy if I buy this? Is it worth giving up those things?

Do I want to take a chance and wait to buy this? It may be on sale later in the season. On the other hand, it may be gone.

Can I buy this for less money at a special store or with a coupon?

Is this something I want as a top priority?

If you get in the habit of asking yourself these questions, it can help you to be a wise money spender. Then, when you decide to buy something, make sure you enjoy it.

Want Something? Get Creative!

People spend money on many different items and services.
If you think creatively, you can probably come up with ways to spend less,
but still enjoy yourself and get the things you want.

Make a trade. You already know about trading. If there's something  you want, can you think of how you might get it through a trade?

 **Make a gift.** Do you know someone who has a birthday coming up? Instead of buying them something from a store, you can make them something special or do something for them that they can enjoy. Handmade gifts come from your heart and will certainly make people happy.

Write down three gifts that you can make for free (or will cost less to make than a store-bought gift):

1. .... 2. .... 3. ....

Having fun doesn't have to cost a lot. Lots of activities cost money. Going to the movies, skating rink, and carnival can be fun, but they also require cash. Creative people can come up with lots of ways to have fun with friends and family without spending any money. Unscramble the words and fill in the blanks to see some ideas below.

Go for a .... ride or a .... You can have fun and get fit at the same time.
　　　　　kbie　　　　　　　lawk

Spend some time in the .... reading or listening to stories.
　　　　　　　　　　　　braliry

You can also enjoy a sport, visit a museum, or find events in your community.

Can you think of other places to go or activities to do that you enjoy and that are also free? ....

Another way to use money is to share it with others. When you do this, you are making your money matter!

When you wish to make the world a better place and then you do something to make that wish come true, that's charity. People who do this are also called "philanthropists."

Charity is happening all over the world. Many cultures and religions have traditions of giving to charity.

There are lots of ways to be a philanthropist— one way is to share your money to help other people. Giving your time, support, and love are also great ways to be a philanthropist. Everyone has something to give, no matter how much money they have.

It's never too early to start thinking of how you can help others and make the world a better place by sharing your money and kind actions.

Your Wishes for Others

A great way to start thinking about how YOU want to share your money is to think about your wishes for others and the world around you.

 Maybe you want to help make the world more peaceful.

 Maybe you want to help people who are sick.

 Maybe you wish the world were cleaner and less polluted.

 Maybe you think everyone should get a chance to learn how to read and write.

 Maybe you want to help people who don't have homes.

 Maybe you hope to help people who can't see or walk or who have other special needs.

List the things that you wish everyone in the world could have and the things that you think would make the world a better place.

....

....

....

Money can be used to buy things that help solve these problems. When people share their money, it brings us closer to making these wishes come true.

Your Charity Priorities

You probably have a lot of wishes for other people and the world.

Just like you need to set priorities for SPENDING money,
it's also wise to set priorities for GIVING money.

What are the top three things that you want to focus on when you give your money to charity?

1. .... 2. .... 3. ....

Great! Now you have a clear idea about your giving priorities. Remember, there's no wrong answer and your priorities might change over time.

Everyone has his or her own ideas about giving. Learn about someone else's wishes and giving priorities. Ask a parent, friend, or relative this question and write their answers below.

What are your top priorities for giving and why?

Giving to charity is a personal decision and
always special because it comes from the heart.

Be a Philanthropist!

You can play a part in making your wishes come true
by donating some of your money to charity.

Some people share 10% of their money. Other people share more or less.
It's up to each person to decide how much to give to charity.

No matter how much you give, it makes a difference! It gets added to
everyone else's money, and when you put it all together, it can add up to a lot!

After deciding on your giving priorities, the next thing to do as a wise
philanthropist and a good planner is to think about how much of your
money you want to set aside to give to others. It's okay if you decide
to be giving in other ways, like volunteering or doing kind deeds.

You and everyone else have a limited amount of money. When you
consider how much you want to give to charity, don't forget that
you'll also want money to save and to spend.

Keep Track of Your Giving

You can keep track of all the good things you do with the money you share!

When you donate your money to help people, list it here.

Date: ....

Who you helped:

....

Why you made that choice:

....

....

....

Date: ....

Who you helped:

....

Why you made that choice:

....

....

....

Date: ....

Who you helped: ....

Why you made that choice: ....

....

You can make copies of this page or create your own
"charity journal" to keep track of your giving.

Other Great Ways to Give

Money is not the only thing you have that can help others. Sometimes we own things—old things, new things—that would be nice to share or give away to other people who might need them.

Here are some other ways to be giving:

Collect all the clothes that you've outgrown. Clean them, fold them, put them in a box, and bring them to the Salvation Army, Goodwill, the Red Cross, or another place that will send them to people who need clothes.

Every once in a while, take one of your old toys—or even one of your new toys or presents—and donate it to an organization that will give it to a child who doesn't have toys.

Donate the books that you don't read anymore to your local library. That way other people can enjoy reading them, too!

Sometimes schools or places of worship have food drives to collect canned goods for people who are hungry. Ask a parent if you have extra food in your cabinets that you could give to people who need it.

You can even organize your family to go through the house to collect other items that you might want to give away to other people.

Your Actions Make a Difference, too!

Another way to give to others is through
KIND and **CARING** actions!

- If you know someone who is lonely or sad, visit them so that they can feel your love and care.

- If you wish the world were cleaner and less polluted, go outside with your parents or friends and pick up trash or help plant a garden.

- If you're a good reader, read stories to someone who can't read. You can even help someone learn how to read.

- If you know a lot about something—like a different language, a subject at school, or a game—teach others about it. Teaching is a great way to share a part of yourself.

There are so many ways that you can be kind and help people EVERY DAY!

SAVING MONEY

An important part of being wise about money matters is to be smart and thoughtful about saving money.

Why save money?

- To have enough to buy the things that you want in the future.

- To donate to charity and help others.

- To start a good habit. Learning to be a smart saver now will help you in money matters for your whole life.

Some people find it easy to save.
Others want to spend all of their money as soon as they get it.
It IS smart to save!!! It is also important to have balance
between the money you save, spend, and share.

And, of course, having savings goals will help you in your
overall money management plans.

Sample Savings Plans

When you have money, how much of it should you save, spend, and give?

Everyone needs to decide the answer to that question based on what their life is like, their values, and their needs and wants. Often someone's answer changes at different times in his or her life.

Work with an adult to figure out how much money goes into each money bag for the two sample savings plans below.

Susan has $100 in savings. In her plan, she wants to put aside money in this way: 30% to spend (to buy something she wants now or very soon); 30% for short-term savings (for something she wants to buy for herself or as a present for someone in the next couple of months); 40% for long-term savings (for something she knows she wants in the future—like a car or money for college).

$ _____ $ _____ $ _____

John also has $100. He wants to spend a third, save a third, and give a third to charity. A third is 33.3%. How much money goes into each money bag with his plan?

SPEND   SAVE   GIVE

$ _____ $ _____ $ _____

What's YOUR Plan?

Now it's your turn to think about your savings plan
and the balance that feels right to you.

Pretend someone just gave you $100. Which of the banks below do
you want to add money to? How much do you want to put in each?

Money to spend soon

$ ....

What will you spend it on?

....

....

....

Money for charity

$ ....

What charity or cause do you want to give this to?

....

....

....

Money for short-term savings

$ ....

Is there something you are saving to buy?

....

....

....

Money for long-term savings

$ ....

What is your top long-term savings goal (something big you want to start saving for that seems important in your future)?

....

....

....

Your savings plan can change as your goals change. For example, pretend your
mother's birthday is coming up and you want to save money to buy her a present.
To help save up for her gift, you may put less money in your spending bank and
more money in your short-term savings bank for a while.

What's important is to keep each of these banks
in mind when you have money.

Create Your Own Banks

Do you have any money saved?

To help stay organized in your savings plan, you can create special banks and mark them with labels that say "Money for Now," "Charity," "Short-term Savings," and "Long-term Savings." You can also make any other labels that reflect your savings plan.

Design each of your savings banks so that they look different.
You can draw pictures, glue on magazine images, or write words
that show how you plan to use the money inside each bank.
Do whatever you want to make them feel special!

To get started, draw a couple of your favorite ideas below.

Now that you have your ideas, ask an adult to help you find some boxes, jars, or bags to create these banks.

By making these banks, you'll be using a great savings trick—putting your money away! Now you won't be tempted to spend it all the time.

Spotlight on Savings

A great way to learn even more about saving is to interview people.
Grab a pencil and imagine that you are a reporter. Sit down with a parent, teacher,
or other adult and write down their responses to the questions below.

The News

SUNDAY, MARCH 26

VOL. III, NUMBER IV

How old were you when you started saving money?

What were some of the things that you saved money for and why?

What are three of the most important things that you save money for these days? Why?

How do you feel when you finally reach a savings goal?

What advice can you give me about saving money?

Earning and Growing Money

Throughout your life you will want to have and use money, so now it's time to think about how you might EARN it!

Earning money means that in exchange for putting in your time and energy (work), you get payment (money).

Even though it's great to get a paycheck, working can also provide other rewards. When you work, you can learn new things, meet new people, and gain confidence. If you plan well and really think about it, it's possible to get a job when you are older that will give you money and also give you satisfaction and enjoyment.

Earning through work is the way most people get their money. Another way people increase their money is by investing it. You'll learn a little bit about that in this chapter, too.

Working Now

You might have some money saved up or get an allowance. But what can you do if you don't have as much money as you want in your plan to spend, give, and save? **EARN IT!**

Even at your age there may be a lot of ways you can earn some extra money.

FOR HIRE

Here are some kid-friendly jobs: dog-walking, babysitting, doing yard work, selling your art, running a lemonade stand, washing cars, shoveling snow, collecting and returning recyclable bottles.

Now that you are thinking, get creative and write down some more job ideas here:

....

....

....

....

Talk to your mom or dad about your job ideas and see what they think. Maybe together you can come up with a plan for you to earn some money for you to spend, give, and save.

Working in the Future

There are SO many different jobs that adults can do
to earn money and feel good about themselves.

Find some job titles in the puzzle below:

```
C B A T R Q U F C N
A N C E X U D I P A
R I C A C T O R R H
P S O C G P C E E K
E T U H F O T F S G
N A N E D W O I I A
T J T R L T R G D F
E B A N K E R H E M
R O N P I L O T N P
A R T I S T J E T Q
I E W R I T E R B W
```

WORDS:

- ACCOUNTANT
- ACTOR
- ARTIST
- BANKER
- CARPENTER
- DOCTOR
- FIREFIGHTER
- PILOT
- PRESIDENT
- TEACHER
- WRITER

What do YOU want to do?

Do you know what kind of work you'd like to do when you get older?

When I grow up, I think I would like to be a/an

.... or ....

Now, see if you can learn a little more about those jobs and what it takes to get them.
Ask your parent or teacher to help you find someone who does each of those jobs.
Then you can interview those people and write their answers below.

PERSON'S JOB:_____	PERSON'S JOB:_____
What do you do at work?_____ _____	What do you do at work?_____ _____
What do you like most about your job? _____	What do you like most about your job? _____
What kind of education did you need to get your job?_____ _____	What kind of education did you need to get your job?_____ _____
What other kinds of training helped you get your job?_____ _____	What other kinds of training helped you get your job?_____ _____

Now that you know a bit more about these jobs, you can start thinking
about ways to get prepared to earn money when you are older.

One smart way to plan ahead for any job is to work hard in school now.
If you do your best and stay in school, you will improve your chances
of getting the job you want when you're an adult.

Growing Your Money

Most adults—and even some kids—put their money
into a savings account at a bank.

A savings account is a good way to help you save and keep track of your money.
It helps you save because your money is at the bank and not in your pocket.
That way you won't be tempted to spend your money all the time. Putting your
money in a bank also helps you keep track of it. That's because the bank keeps
records of how much money you put in and take out. The bank also gives you
a passbook where you can write down all of your transactions.

There's another great reason to put
your money in a bank. While your
money sits in the bank, it will GROW!

This happens because the bank pays you to store your money with them.
They add small amounts of money to your savings account. The extra
money they give you is called "interest."

For example, pretend you start a savings account with $100. Even if you don't
add any more of your own money into the account, you can have $103 at the end
of the year. The more money you put in your savings account, and the longer you
leave it there, the more money the bank will give you. Over time, it adds up!

More Ways to Grow Your Money

There are other ways that adults use their money to make more money—it's called investing.

Some types of investing are considered "safe" and some are more "risky."

An investment is considered *safe* when people are pretty sure they'll get all of their money back (plus a bit more that they will earn). In fact, in some safe investments, there's even a guarantee. An investment is *risky* when people aren't as sure that they'll get their money back or that they will earn extra money. But, if their investment does work out, there's a good chance that they'll earn more money than they could have with a safe investment.

Here are just a few examples of ways people invest:

● **Certificates of Deposit (CDs)** Like savings accounts, CDs are a way for people to save and grow their money at the same time. When someone buys a CD, they promise to leave their money in the bank for a number of months or years. In return, the bank promises to give that person a certain amount of interest. CDs are a safe investment.

Do you think you'd like to invest in a CD one day?............... If you earned $50 in interest from a CD, what would you do with it? ....

● **Stocks** When people buy stock, they are buying a tiny piece of a company. Imagine someone bought stock in a toy company. If that company made a great game that sold millions of copies, the company would likely make money—and the investor would, too! But if the company came out with a game that no one wanted to buy, the company and the investor might lose money. Since no one can be 100% sure of how a company will do, investing in stocks can be risky.

Do you think you'd like to invest in stocks one day?............... If so, write down three companies that you'd invest in and why. ....

....

● **Collectibles** Another way people use their money to make more money is by collecting. That means they buy something today that they think will be worth more money in the future. People buy and resell all sorts of things, like baseball cards, comic books, autographs, paintings, cars, and much more! But collecting can be risky, too. Sometime collectibles turn out to be worth less money than an investor hoped.

Do you think you'd like to invest in collectibles one day? .... If so, what sorts of things do you think it might be profitable—and fun—to collect? ....

....

....

....

If you want to learn more about investing, ask your mom or dad about super savings accounts, bonds, and mutual funds. These are other tools to help people grow their money.

If you learn anything that you think is important about investing, you can write about it here: ....

....

....

....

....

Investing can be complicated. That's why some adults ask experts to help them manage their money.

YOUR BUDGET

You've worked your way through the
whole book and now you know a lot about

SPENDING MONEY, GIVING MONEY, SAVING MONEY, EARNING MONEY, AND GROWING MONEY.

Now it's time to bring it ALL TOGETHER!

Wise money managers like you know that all of these money matters are connected and need to be balanced in a financial PLAN.

A great tool to help people see their whole plan is a BUDGET.

Budgets help you keep an eye on the balance between how much money comes in and goes out of your life every month.

When you see these amounts, you can decide if you are meeting your goals and managing your money matters wisely.

You will also see that you always have choices. When you want to change the balance, you can decide to spend, give, save, and earn more or less money to achieve your goals.

's Budget

First, write down how much money you **get each month.** Include any money you get from allowance, working, or gifts. Add it all together and you get your "expected income." (You might not get the same amount every month. And there may be some months that you don't get any money.)

Total Expected Income: $ _____

Next, write down the things you know you **will spend money on.** These are called "expenses." For adults this section would begin with money to spend on family needs (like rent, heat, car, etc.). For you, it might include something you want to buy for yourself or someone else, or money you want to give to charity this month. You can only spend money that you have, so get in the important habit of making sure that this number is LESS than your expected income!

Total Expenses: $ _____

Now, subtract what you will spend (expenses) **from what you will earn** (expected income) **and you will see how much you will have left to save this month.**

Total Savings: $ _____

One Last Budget Step: The final—and very important—step is to ANALYZE your budget.

That's when you think about your results and see if they match your goals.

To analyze your results, look at how much money you've saved and ask yourself if you are happy with that amount. (As you consider your answer, remember your short-term, medium-term, and long-term savings goals.)

If you are pleased with the amount you have saved, then you have a good and balanced budget. Great!

If you want to save more, then you can make some decisions. You can either spend less money or you can try to earn more money.

Keeping a Budget!

Now that you have experience creating your first budget, KEEP IT UP!

Keeping a budget is a great habit and will help you remain a wise money manager!

OTHER STUFF

YAY YOU!

Congratulations!

This NICKELS, DIMES, AND DOLLARS BOOK certificate
shows that you have learned a lot about money and
how you can manage it now and throughout your life.

#1

THE NICKELS, DIMES, AND DOLLARS BOOK

This certificate is awarded to

....

WRITE YOUR NAME HERE

for being a wise money manager.

....

DATE

Now that you know how great it feels to spend, share, save, earn, and
grow money wisely, keep it up. Remember, you can make decisions
that put you in charge of your money matters.

Join Watering Can® Press in growing kids with character.

www.wateringcanpress.com

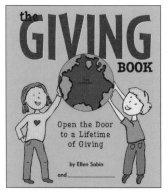

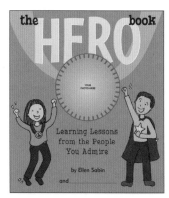

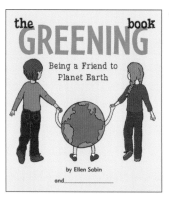

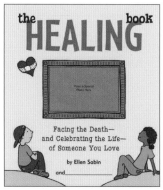

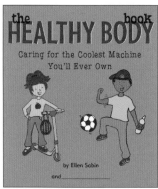

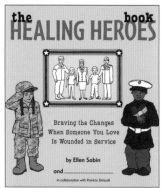

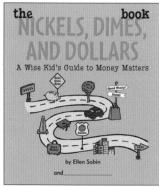

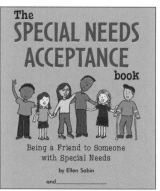

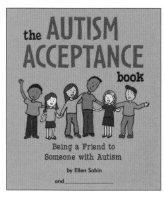

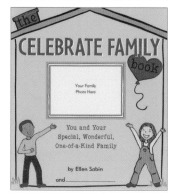

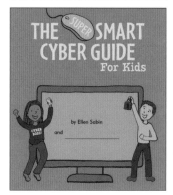

- Order our other books and enjoy a 15% discount using promo code *"life."*
- Learn about bulk discounts and branded versions for organizations.
- Explore Author Events for your students, clients, employees, or community.
- View the **FREE** Teacher's Guides and Parent's Guides available on our site.

We hope you've learned
a lot about money matters and
the smart choices you can make
to spend, share, save, earn,
and grow your money.